ATTILA BONHARDT

40M NIMRÓD TANK DESTROYER AND ARMOURED ANTI AIRCRAFT GUN

ARMOUR OF THE ROYAL HUNGARIAN ARMY

Published by
PeKo Publishing Kft.
8360 Keszthely, Bessenyei György utca 37., Hungary
Email: info@pekobooks.com
www.pekobooks.com

Responsible publisher
Péter Kocsis

Author
Attila Bonhardt

Editing
Jon Feenstra

First Published
2019

ISBN 978-615-5583-14-8

THE UTILIZATION OF THE L-62 TANK-HUNTER AND SELF-PROPELLED ANTI-AIRCRAFT AUTOCANNON IN THE ROYAL HUNGARIAN ARMY

When the representatives of the Royal Hungarian Army (Magyar Királyi Honvédség) got familiar with the L-60 light tank of the Swedish AB Landswerk Company in a presentation with film screening on 3rd December 1936, their hosts also presented them with a self-propelled 40 mm anti-aircraft autocannon built on the same chassis as the vehicle mentioned above. The Swedish designers described the L-62 as a tank-hunter.

Both vehicles – but especially the tank-hunter version – attracted the attention of the Hungarian Military leaders. The Chief of Staff of the Royal Hungarian Army believed that the L-62 could be employed as a support vehicle mostly with the quick mobile units (cavalry, bicycle infantry, motorized rifle units and the newly raised armoured units) primarily in an anti-aircraft role, secondly in an anti-tank role. The speed and cross-country capabilities of the tracked vehicle could keep up with the tanks and provide protection to the advancing troops against the attacks of the enemy's aircraft and tanks at the same time.

Still in the same year a Hungarian military committee travelled to Landskrona, Sweden to determine if the L-60 light tank and L-62 tank-hunter:

1. would met the Hungarian military and technical requirements,
2. could be produced in Hungary,
3. and would the committee recommend the utilization of the vehicles after considering the above mentioned aspects?[1]

As a result of the positive assessment of the committee and the succesful trials, the MÁVAG (Magyar Állami Vas-, Acél- és Gépgyárak Rt. – Royal Hungarian State Iron, Steel and Machine Factory Ltd.) and the GANZ-Factory (Ganz & Co. Danubius Electricity, Machine, Waggon and Shipyards Ltd) bought the licences of the L-60 light tank and prepared for the domestic production of the vehicle. As the chassis of the L-62 tank-hunter was the same as the L-60 light tank and the tank-hunter's 40 mm Bofors anti-aircract autocannon was already licensed in Hungary it seemed to be obvious to put into service both of them. The 40 mm anti-aircraft autocannon of the self-propelled gun met the requirements of the general staff as it was effective against both ground and aerial targets. Since MÁVAG could now expect a significiant order from the Honvédség, they bought one L-62 and the manufacturing licence of the vehicle in 1937.[2]

The sample vehicle arrived to Hungary in December 1938, without armament. It was transferred to Diósgyőr, where a domestically produced 40 mm Bofors anti-aircraft autocannon was mounted on it. Right after this the vehicle was handed over to the army for presentation and trials.[3]

The difference between the chassis of the self-propelled gun and the L-60 tank (which was utilized in the Royal Hungarian Army as Toldi) was that the former had five pairs of roadwheels instead of four. However, the new wheels were smaller in diameter and the new vehicle's chassis became 0,66 m longer. Naturally the superstructure differed from a tank's superstructure. The autocannon and the four crewmen were placed in a truncated conical, rotating turret, which was made of 6-10 mm thick armour plate. There were openings in the front and both sides of the turret for the aiming devices. These openings and the open top of the turret made possible the leveling of the barrel between -5 and 90 degrees. The only difference between the vehicle's cannon and the original 36M. 40 mm Bofors anti-aircraft cannon was that the legs of the cross base were shortened and placed on the floor plate of the turret. The fifth member of the

1 Hadtörténelmi Levéltár (Military Archive – HL) Chief of Staff of the Royal Hungarian Army (VKF) 1757/eln.VI-1.-1936.

2 HL VKF 2179/eln.1.-1937., VKF 9180/Hr.1.-1938.

3 HL Honvédelmi Minisztérium (HM) 29713/eln.e.b.-1942 alapszám, 92713/eln.3.b.-1938. ikt.szám

crew (the driver) sat in the cramped driver's compartment in the left front of the vehicle which hosted the instruments and the steering wheel. It shows how small the driver's compartment was in that the driver (just like the driver of the TOLDI) could get out of the vehicle through the hatch above his seat only if he removed the steering wheel by pulling out a pin, and placing it into a cavity designed specifically for this purpose. The steering unit was controlled by a steering wheel just like in the case of the TOLDI tank. The sum of this solution is that a planetary speed reducer slows down the speed of the track on the side where the steering wheel is turned, while the other side's track runs at higher speed. In this way the vehicle would turn to the slower track's direction. The disadvantage of this solution against the clutch brake system is that the tracks couldn't be completely stopped during turning, so the L-62 couldn't make a pivot turn; its turning radius was 10 meters.

The demonstration of the L-62 self-propelled anti-aircraft autocannon to the leadership – where the Chief of Staff also appeared – took place on 30th March 1939.[4] As a result, field tials were ordered.

During the field trials in August 1939, the L-62 was examined from both a technical and an artillery point of view. During the life-like trials the self-propelled gun reached 50km/h speeds on roads with its German-made 155HP 8-cylinder Büssing engine. Its cross-country mobility also proved to be good: it could cross a 2,2 m wide ditch, climbed up a 35-40 degree slope and could fell a 30 cm diameter tree without stopping. It is interesting to note that the steereing mechanism was found to be good – unlike in the case of the TOLDI. The relevant part of the report says: 'The current solution of steering is appropriate for a vehicle with this weight and size. When comparing steering lever and wheel, the latter seems more suitable. Justification: the re-training of civilian drivers would be more simple, and the steering wheel performs its task just as well as the steering lever.' Only the stop arm of the idler wheel and the torsion bars were found slightly weak. In summary it was found that the self-propelled gun (as a vehicle) could follow the infantry everywhere, and would not lag behind the mobile units thanks to its high speed.

The artillery officers were pleased to say that with the appearance of the 36M 40 mm self-propelled anti-aircraft cannon the air-defence of the mobile troops (which didn't exist before) was finally solved. Namely, a constantly combat-ready vehicle which could move along with the mechanized troops and could shoot at the suddenly appearing aerial targets anytime. The towed artillery was unable to do such a thing because getting into position was time consuming.

The tests found that the L-62 was a full value anti-aircraft weapon, although it couldn't be mounted with all of the instruments because of the small size of the crew. Because of this, the L-62 couldn't apply all of the procedures which the same anti-aircraft cannon could (ie. the 36M. 40 mm Bofors anti-aircraft cannon). Based on the experience gained during the tests, the artillery experts recommended that an additional member be added to the 4 man crew of the L-62's autocannon. This was found necessary because the gunner couldn't adjust the predictor during the fight as he was busy with following the target. In order to accomodate a fifth person in the already cramped turret, it was suggested that the rounded turret could be extended backwards. To increase the internal space, they suggested changing the conical sides of the turret into vertical armour plates. They also recommended increasing the front armour's height by 28 cm to protect against the aerial attacks and also to widen the sighting ports in the turret.

They also suggested the utilization of a vehicle on the same chassis and superstructure but with fixed turret for that case when the L-62 had to engage enemy aircraft from fixed positions. The vehice would carry a telemeter (the same one which was utilized for the anti-aircraft cannon half-platoon) and a target element measuring instrument in the turret. In action these instruments would be used outside the vehicle. The new vehicle's crew would be the radio-group and the vehicle would also serve as an ammunition carrier. It would be armed with a heavy machine gun (on the front) and two light machine guns (on the sides) which would be operated by the crew. It was believed that the L-62 would be equivalent to the air-defense troop's anti-aircraft cannons in this way.

The gun was tested against ground targets too. The bouncing caused by the shooting (120 rounds/minute) didn't influence the dispersion. Only the representatives of the armoured branch graded the gun sighting device too complicated during anti-tank engagements. They requested a more simple sighting device which could be used by one person.

All in all, the experts taking part in the trials concluded that the L-62 fully met the anti-aircraft and anti-tank roles' requirements of the mechanized troops, and they

4 HL VKF 3575/eln.1.-1939.

recommended the utilization of the fighting vehicle after making the suggested modifications.[5]

The Institute of Military Technology received all these opinions and suggestions, and carefully considered them. They admitted the necessity of the fifth crew member. The rounded layout of the turret was lengthened and the end of the turret closed with a vertical armour plate. In this increased turret they managed to placed the fifth member of the crew. The height of the front plates of the turret were also increased. But the suggestion of the simpler ground aiming device was rejected. According to the requirements of the General Staff they emphasized that the self-propelled gun must be effective against both aerial and ground targets – but only the original aiming equipment is suitable against aerial targets. Any change to other equipment would disrupt the operational commonality of the gun.

The Institute of Military Technology thought that the tank officers disliked the equipment which was well-proven in the air-defense role because they were unfamiliar with it. They rejected the idea of the vertical sidewalls of the turret which was intended to increase the inner space, because this would have reduced the protection of the vehicle. They also rejected the utilization of the recommended armoured tracked carrier for the air-defence instruments and their crew because of financial reasons. They explained in their justification that the self-propelled cannon could perform its task without the mentioned instruments both against ground and aerial targets. These would only be needed in fixed position, but in that case they could use those instruments which were normally carried by the unit's other utilized vehicles.

The Institute of Military Technology ended its explanation with the directive for the self-propelled guns developed in England. According to this, the self-propelled guns had to attack in the third wave and support the tanks in the first wave. As assumed, the tanks would destroy the enemy's anti-tank weapons, so the self-propelled guns only have to face the sporadic resistance of the infantry. Due to these arguments, the Institute considered the 6-13 mm armour protection of the L-62 sufficient (which provides protection against only small caliber infantry weapons and splinters), and ignored the fact that the L-62 was to be used not only as a self-propelled anti-aircraft vehicle, but also as a tank-hunter, which unavoidably led to fights against heavily armed tanks.

5 HL HM 13457/eln.3.b.-1940.

Based on the above, the Institute of Military Technology suggested the utilization of the L-62 in the Royal Hungarian Army and urged the order of a prototype from MÁVAG with the recommended modifications.

Based on field trials and the opinion of the Institute of Military Technology, the L-62 was utilized in the Hungarian army in May 1940 as 40 mm 40M. NIMRÓD tank-hunter and anti-aircraft cannon.

The tank-hunter units were included with the armoured branch, because 'the vehicle's maintenance would already be known due to the TOLDI tank'.[6]

ORDERS OF NIMRÓD

Although the MÁVAG already had the licence of the L-62 at the beginning of 1940, the company couldn't start the production because they didn't buy the necesssary technical drawings, since the tracing paper (which would be suitable for making copies) cost 30000 Swedish crowns. The Hungarian company didn't want more expenses until they received an order for the vehicles.

According to the warning of the Institute of Military Technology (that the preparation of the technical drawings would take 3-4 months[7]), the Ministry of Defense ordered a prototype from MÁVAG on 19th March 1940 before the utilization of the vehicle with the promise that more orders would follow. The MÁVAG bought the drawings forthwith so that copies were ready in July 1940.[8] When the drawings were available, and the company was ready to manufacture the vehicle on the basis of their experiencies with the TOLDI tank, the Ministry of Defense ordered 46 NIMRÓD (original design with modified turret) in September 1940[9].

The first order was followed by a new one for 89 tank-hunters in July 1941.[10] The vehicles of the new batch (called NIMRÓD II series) looked similar to the first batch's vehicles, except for one significant difference. The shipping of the Büssing-NAG engines from

6 HL VKF 3412/eln.1.-1940.
7 HL VKF 3412/eln.1.-1940.
8 HL HM 18011/3eln.3.b.-1941., HM 37162/eln.3.b.-1940.
9 HL HM 11690/eln.3.b.-1941. alapszám, 39973/eln.3.b.-1941. iktatószám
10 HL HM 43429/eln.3.b.-1941. alapszám, 488436eln.3.b.-1941. iktatószám

Germany was precarious so the second batch of NIMRÓD was ordered with domestically produced GANZ VIII. VGT 107 engine which had similar performance.[11] The MÁVAG was relieved from participation in the TOLDI III. programme and the production of the heavy 'TURAN' because the company was charged with the complete manufacturing of 135 NIMRÓD.

The first Hugnarian made NIMRÓD left the factory in October 1941.[12]

Because of the modification to the turret the original dimensons changed: length – 5,32 m; width – 2,3 m; height – 2,8 m. The combat weight increased to 10,5 t which put more load on the already weak torsion bars.

The production was relatively continuous except for the installation of the radio equipment, because at the start of the production there was no clear concept about the air-defense role of the NIMRÓD. As there were suppositions that the self-propelled anti-aircraft cannons would operate independently, there wouldn't be a need for a consolidated fire control system. Nevertheless the command of the training camp of the air-defense artillery insisted that the 'tank-hunter' units must be fitted with the most necessary equipment (1,25 m rangefinder, target-measuring instruments), because they can't operate without these. That's why the leadership recommended the utilization of a truck for every platoon (2 NIMRÓDs) to carry the measuring tools of the unit.

The recommendation was accepted during a meeting on 31st January 1941.[13] Thereafter they developed the communication system of the NIMRÓD platoons. The connection between the crew inside the NIMRÓD and the fire-control crew's station (which was to be deployed within 60 m) was provided by a wired communication and fire-control system. The measured data was transmitted via throat-microphone, and was received by the NIMRÓD's crew by a loudspeaker placed in the turret. The fire-control commander in the turret also had a throat-microphone so he could keep in contact with the fire-control station.

11 HL HM 548445/3b.-1943 és HM 566204/3b.-1943.
12 HL HM 73198/eln.3.b.-1941.
13 HL HM 14766/eln.3.b.-1941.

The fire-control commander could communicate with the driver by throat-microphone during march. The driver received the instructions both on his helmet's earphone and by a loudspeaker placed beside him.

The communication between the unit commander and the unit's vehicles was maintained by a R/5 radio installed into the turret on the right side of the rear wall in every NIMRÓD. Usually the radio was handled by the fire-control commander, except during shooting, when the driver handled it.[14]

The trial of the experimental radio equipment of the NIMRÓD took place in August 1941, and production started in October, when the first tank-hunters were handed over. That's why the shipping of some spare parts (amplifiers, loudspeakers, outer cables, plugs) was undertook by STANDARD Villamossági Rt. only from April 1942 – right after the end of the NIMRÓD's first batch.[15]

NIMRÓD SHIPPING

The first batch of NIMRÓD[16]

Period	6.41	7.41	8.41	9.41	10.41	11.41	12.41	1.42	2.42	3.42	4.42	5.42
To be handed over according to the original plans			1		5	6	6	6	6	6	4	
To be handed over according to the accelerated plans	1		5	8	8	8	8	8				
Completed vehicles					1	10	16				10	9
Shipped vehicles					1	11	27				37	46

Note: The handover of those 27 NIMRÓDs which were completed in 1941 took place in February – March 1942 because of the weather conditions. The shipping of the remaining 19 vehicles was hindered for a few months by the shortages of the tires and the delay of the spare parts coming from abroad.

14 Technical manual of the fire-control system and radio instruments of the NIMRÓD.
15 HL HM 73198/eln.3.b.-1941.
16 HM 852/eln.III.Csf-1942., HM 11690/eln.3.b.-1941. alapszám 39973/eln.3.b.-1942. iktatószám

The second batch of NIMRÓD[17]

Period	2.43	3.43	4.43	5.43	6.43	7.43	8.43	9.43	10.43	11.43	12.43	1.44	2.44	3.44	4.44	5.44
To be handed over according to the original plans	6	6	6	6	6	6	6	6	6	6	6	6	6	6	5	
To be handed over according to the accelerated plans	6	6	6	6	9	9	9	9	9	9	9	5				
Completed vehicles			9	2	13	3	12	12	9	5	7	6		5		6
Shipped vehicles			9	11	24	27	39	51	60	65	72	78		83		89

Note: The second batch of NIMRÓD was overshadowed by the TURAN programme, and caused delays until the summer of 1942. That's why there was a one-year break between the first and second batch.

CONTROVERSIES ABOUT THE DEPLOYMENT OF THE NIMRÓD

The Hungarian military leadership followed the deployment of the Weharmacht's tanks during the Polish and French campaign with close attention. Lieutenant-Colonel Ferenc Koszorús of the General Staff evaluated the Hungarian armoured branch on the basis of German military experiencies in his study of 'Armoured corps and armour defense'. About the NIMRÓD, he wrote: 'The primary duty of this self-propelled, lightly armoured autocannon is to provide fire protection for the advancing waves of the armoured forces against tanks… enforce the weight of fire in the main point of attack. This is specifically a supporting weapon and also the main tool of the air-defense.' Lieutenant-Colonel Koszorús appreciated the 120 round/minute rate of fire of the autocannon against the single shot tank guns. In his study he compared the role of the tank-hunters with the role of the machinegun companies of the infantry battalions. He was only dissatisfied with the armour-piercing ability of the NIMRÓD. In his opinion he stated that the armour-piercing round had to penetrate 50 mm armour within 1000 meters at 60 degrees. In contrast, the 40 mm autocannon could penetrate this thickness only within 80 meters. He recommended the increase of the cannon's caliber to 50 mm.[18]

The General Staff rejected the utilization of the 50 mm caliber. They emphasized that the main role of the tank-hunter vehicle was armour defense in lieu of the towed anti-tank guns in the line of the fast-troops and substitution of the towed anti-aircraft artillery within the armoured troops. The 40 mm autocannon met both tasks. In case the armoured troops had to fight against tanks, the weight of the fighting would be born by heavy tanks armed with 75 mm guns.[19]

There was a clear reason for this denial. The complete NIMRÓD program was based on a well proven weapon-system: the domestically made BOFORS anti-aircraft autocannon with the 40 mm ammunition which was also produced in Hungary and was used for several guns. Altought the increased caliber would have increased the armour-piercing ability, it would have been an unsolvable problem both in gun and ammunintion production.

Despite the clear resolution of the General Staff, the name 'tank-hunter' continously caused problems. According to its name the armoured troops wanted to deploy the tank-hunters in the first wave of the tank attacks against armoured targets and anti-tank weapons. They completely ignored the fact that the 13 mm armour of the NIMRÓD could provide protection against only infantry weapons so it was absolutely unsuitable for this task. At the same time they didn't pay enough attention to the air-defense abilities of the NIMRÓD. According to the 4th (training) department of the General Staff 'the air-defense, the anti-tank defense and to defeat the enemy's anti-tank weapons should be equally important tasks for the tank-hunter units of the armoured troops'. The department thought it was evident that the weakly armoured tank-hunters shouldn't be used in the first wave or in front of it, because it would lead to its complete destruction. In their opinion the NIMRÓDs were to be employed in the second line of the first attacking wave, where they can perform both of their important tasks: the air-defense and the anti-tank defense.

17 HL HM 852/eln.III.Csf.-1942.; HM 23366/eln.3.b.-1943. alapszám 23753, 29928, 36174, 38807/eln.3b.-1943 iktatószám; 49857/eln.3.b.-1943. alapszám, 58016, 63990, 64067, 71598,69747, 778657/ eln.3.b.-1943. iktatószám; Hadianyaggyártás hadbiztossága 3335/1944, 4518/1944, 7149/1944.
No shipping dates available between May – October 1943. In this case we present the dates when the units received the vehicles.

18 HL VKF 4997/eln.1.-1940.; VKF 5128/eln.1.-1940.
19 HL VKF 5128/eln.1.-1940.

The 1. (preparatory) department of the General Staff had a different opinion. As they explained it, they would give the task of air-defense to the tank-hunter units of the armoured troops, because the tank unit could parry the tank attacks. Because the misunderstanding was caused by the name, the department recommended renaming the NIMRÓD as 40 mm 36M. armoured air-defense autocannon as soon as the Order of Battle for 1942/1943 come into effect (from October 1942 onward).[20] Later they specified the name as 40 mm 36/40 armoured air-defense autocannon, to avoid the confusion with the towed 36M. air-defense autocannon.[21]

In February 1942 the 3. (hand-held and artillery weapons) department of the Ministry of Defense requested to reclassify the armoured autocannon units to the branch of the air-defense artillery from the armoured troops (with unchanged deployment), and asked the air-defense artillery branch to provide their crews. The department justified its request that the air-defense artillery crews could use the anti-aircraft cannons without any difficulty both in the air-defense and anti-tank roles. In contrast, the re-training of the armoured troops' officers to handle the NIMRÓD would take too long and would be very difficult. Theoretically the Ministry and the competent departments of the General Staff agreed with the idea. Only the 1.b (order of battle, mobilization) department of the Ministry of Defense had a different point of view. As they said, part of the tank-hunter units were already under mobilization, so any reorganization would lead to a mess.[22] The Chief of the General Staff approved this protest and decided to keep the armoured autocannon units within the fast troops' order of battle until the battle reports arrived.[23]

THE FIRST ACTIONS OF THE ARMOURED AUTOCANNON UNITS AND THEIR REORGANIZATION TO THE AIR-DEFENSE ARTILLERY

The 51. Anti-Tank Battalion of the 1. Armoured Division was sent to the Don battlefield with 18 NIMRÓD (1st batch) in the summer of 1942 (with two more tanks in the field replacement squad). One company with the replacement squad of the battalion stayed in Esztergom. Most likely the missing company was replaced by the 31. Independent Tank Battalion's tank-hunter company.

20 HL VKF 5782/eln.1.-1941.
21 HL VKF 1840/eln.1.-1942.
22 HL VKF 5253/eln.1.-1943. alapszám, 4430/eln.1.-1942. iktatószám
23 HL VKF 5253/eln.1.-1943. alapszám, 5926/eln.1.-1942. iktatószám

According to the summary report of the first months war experiences, the NIMRÓD had proven itself well as an anti-aircraft weapon. It also worked well against the smaller, lightly armoured and weaker armed light tanks (T-60, American made Stuart) against which its higher rate of fire and more precise sightings were superior. The same was true against the enemy's anti-tank weapons and machinegun nests. Neverthless, the NIMRÓD proved inferior against the T-34 and KV-1 tanks – which were appearing in increasing numbers from September 1942 – because of its weaker armour piercing ability. It was proven by tests carried out with a captured T-34. As it was determined, the autocannon could tear away the tracks of the T-34 with bursts from 200 meters, but couldn't pierce the armour.[24] According to the reports, during the battles for the bridgeheads, only once could a NIMRÓD knock out a T-34, when a lucky shot hit the periscope of the enemy's tank. At the same time, the NIMRÓD's high superstructure attracted the attention of the anti-tank guns and tanks very quickly. The Soviet tank-destroyer troops threatened great danger to the open-topped vehicle, when the soldiers approached in the high undergrowth. Thanks only to great luck the 51. Anti-Tank Battalion didn't suffer serious loss during the summer battles (only three vehicles were sent home without armament by October 1942).

Lieutenant-Colonel Törcsváry, the battalion-commander, concluded in his report: 'According to the latest experiences the NIMRÓD in this current state is well suited against aerial targets. However, it is increasingly unfit for anti-tank roles.'[25]

The remaining NIMRÓDs of the 51. tank-hunter battalion had great success while they provided air cover for the retreating troops during the retreat of the Hungarian 2. Army in January – February 1943. With their short and accurate fire bursts they played a major role in containing the pursuing Soviet troops, and to open up the 'bulges' which blocked the way of the Hungarian soldiers. Nevertheless, all of the NIMRÓDs in the operational area, with the exception of the three vehicles which were sent home earlier – were lost due to enemy action or mechanical failure.[26]

The NIMRÓD's failure as a tank-hunter settled the more than year-long debate. During 1943/1944 the armoured autocannons were gradually reorganized into the

24 HL Collection of studies, recollections (Tgy.) 4245/I.
25 HL HM 25805/eln.3.b.-1943.
26 HL, After-action reports of 51. tank-hunter battalion, Royal Hungarian 2. Army; HL TGy. 2974 Barczy Zoltán: A magyar légvédelmi tüzérség fejlődése. Vol. 7, 866. p.

air-defense artillery and they were used as self-propelled air-defense cannons to cover the fast troops.[27]

Of course, the armoured autocannons should be prepared to engage ground targets too. Based on German methods, from 1943 the ammunition stocks of the NIMRÓDs were supplemented with shape-charged shells to help fight against the thickly armoured Soviet tanks. The warhead functions by having the explosive charge collapse a metal liner inside the warhead to form a high-velocity superplastic jet of liquid metal. This concentrated liquid metal jet is capable of penetrating armor steel to a depth of seven or more times the diameter of the charge. Since the caliber of the grenade was bigger than the NIMRÓD's 40 mm autocannon, the so-called stick-grenade was used. The 16 cm diameter mallet-head shell was attached to an approximately 80 cm long shaft and its upper part was surrounded by a perforated cylindrical skirt. As the shaft was pushed into the barrel, the 'skirt' hit the flash suppressor. The cartridge was closed with a paper cap. The biggest disadvantage of this grenade was the short range which was caused by the low muzzle velocity. Its effective range was only 100 meters. The single-shot ability and that it had to be reloaded from outside the vehicle meant further disadvantages. Practically there was no chance to reload the cannon during an engagement.[28]

The last NIMRÓDs of the second batch's 89 vehicles were handed over in the spring of 1944. With these vehicles they gradually filled up the 52. Anti-Tank Battalion of the 2. Armoured Division raised in October 1942, the armoured autocannon platoons of the 1. Tank Regiment and the armoured anti-aircraft autocannon companies (4 vehicles each) of the 6 tank and infantry battalions.[29] Also the 51. Armoured Autocannon Battalion (the renamed 51. Anti-Tank Battalion, which lost its NIMRÓDs at the river Don) was refilled with these new vehicles. Some schools also received a couple of them.

Based on past experiencies the NIMRÓDs were deployed against aerial, unarmoured, or weakly armoured targets in the foreground of the Carpathians in 1944. Most of the armoured anti-aircraft autocannons were destroyed during the battles. Today there are only two NIMRÓDs. One of them was captured by Soviet troops and can be seen in Kubinka Tank Musem (NIMRÓD I). The other one was restored, and today it belongs to the Hungarian Military Museum in operational condition (NIMRÓD II).

27 HL VKF 5253/eln.1.-1943., HM 43000/eln.1.a.-1943.
28 HL TGy. 2974 Barczy Zoltán: A magyar légvédelmi tüzérség fejlődése. Vol. 5, 715/A-B pp.
29 HL HM 42000/eln.1.a-1942.

As a summary it can be stated that the NIMRÓD was an appropriate self-propelled anti-aircraft autocannon. Its biggest 'fault' was the fact that it was used in the anti-tank role for which it was unfit because of its weak armour piercing capabilitiy, high silhouette and weak armour protection.

ARMOURED CARRIERS BASED ON THE CHASSIS OF THE NIMRÓD

Plans for the utilization of an armoured troop carrier

Based on the Wehrmacht campaigns it was clear that the success of the armoured troops could only be achieved by close coorporation with the infantry (more precisely with the mechanized infantry). Based on German war experiences, in 1941 the Hungarian Military Leadership wished for an armoured personnel carrier which could follow the tanks on rough terrain without lagging behind neither in time, nor in space. According to the requirements the vehicle (which had to carry a squad of 15 soldiers and two drivers) had to be equipped with armour protection against small arms fire. The leadership wanted a tracked, or half-tracked solution as required by the cross-country capability.[30]

They decided on domestic purchase, because there were no possibilities of buying from foreign countries – especially because of Germany's refusal. The Institue of Military Technology (responsible for the development of the plans) took a stand on a fighting vehicle based on the NIMRÓD tank-hunter, which was already in production in Hungary. The fact that the Hungarian industry was already prepared to produce the NIMRÓD's chassis also confirmed this proposal. Furthermore, the NIMRÓD's speed and cross-country capability was equal to the TOLDI tank. However, the engine's rear position and the relatively short chassis meant a disadvantage, because there was not enough room for an entire squad. In its first report, the Military Institute considered the vehicle fit for only a half-squad (6 troops) and two drivers.

Despite its benefits, the General Staff didn't consider this solution acceptable, because this would have increased the length of the march columns, not to mention the increasing costs to equip all the units with the vehicles.[31]

30 HL VKF 5385/eln.1.-1941., 6447/eln.1.-1941.; HM 30992/eln.3.b.-1941.
31 HL VKF 5385/eln.1.-1941.

The Institue of Military Technology managed to increase the capacity to eleven, later to twelve by redesigning the plans. The anticipated price of the new vehicle would have been almost the same as the NIMRÓD's price, namely ca. 130 000 pengő. Finally, the Military Leadership cancelled the plan, because the outfit of one battalion with armoured personnel carriers would have costed 17 million pengő. The BOTOND cross-country truck remained the main means of transport of the mechanized infantry battalions.[32]

43M. LEHEL armoured ambulance and troop carrier cross-country vehicle

The topic of armoured personnel carriers was again on the agenda in 1943. According to the experiences learned on the battlefield, the rescue of a knocked out tank's crew within the range of the enemy's firearms was almost impossible without armoured vehicles. The armoured troops requested an armoured ambulance vehicle which could carry the seriously wounded soldiers to the first aid station.[33] Whereas it was still impossible to purchase anything from Germany, the Military Institute received an order to develop the plans for an ambulance vehicle. The Institue presented a vehicle based on the NIMRÓD's chassis once again. According to the plans, the turret would have been replaced with an open-topped, armoured superstructure for the wounded soldiers and the medics. The height of the sidewalls would have been increased, and a door would have been cut into the rear wall for loading. According to the designers, the vehicle would be capable of carrying the sapper-units of the armoured troops as well with only modest conversion.

While there was no directive from the part of the General Staff, the Military Institute made the plans according to the needs of the troops. These were as follows:

1. To strengthen the front of the vehicle with welded armour plates as on the TOLDI III tank.
2. 20 mm protection on the modified part of the hull.
3. Crew:
   - armoured ambulance: 4 stretchers, 2 sitting wounded, 1 medic, 1 driver
   - sapper troop carrier: 7 sappers, 1 driver, 100 kg of demolition charges and technical equipment

32 HL VKF 5743/eln.1.-1941., 6447/eln.1.-1941.; HM 37493/eln.3.b.-1941.
33 HL HM 3173/eln.3.b.-1943.

The plans were ready in May 1943. The Institue of Military Technology received the iron body prototype of the NIMRÓD to build the new prototype. The Ministry of Defense provided 100 000 pengő loan for the experiments with the vehicle.[34]

The transformation of the iron-made NIMRÓD was finished in July 1943 at the MÁVAG. From the perspective of the engine and the chassis, the vehicle was the same as the NIMRÓD. The armour protection of the front and side walls was increased to 20 mm and on the other parts of the vehicle it remained the original 6-13 mm protection. During the rebuilding the number of carried personnel could be increased with one more person in both versions.

The sapper-version (designated as 'Á'; sapper – árkász) carried 8 soldiers and 1 driver. The sappers sat on the folding and removable padded seats on the left and right side of the vehicle.

The ambulance version (designated as 'S'; wounded – sebesült) could carry 4 wounded on stretchers, 1 wounded on the seat and 3 medics. 2 stretchers were placed above each other on both sides. 4 folding seats were placed on the right side of the vehicle. The stretchers were loaded in on rails, fastened to the engine deck at the rear.[35] Regarding the production, the two versions were the same, and their conversion took 10 minutes.

The field trials of the new vehicles were in July 1943. During the tests, new wishes arose which led to necessary redesigning. The most important were: 1) in the case of the ambulance version they wanted the same stretcher as the ones in the Ford ambulance; 2) in the case of the troop carrier they found the seats too small for the troops with their complete personal gear.

According to the Institute of Military Technology's opinion, the problem of the different stretcher could be solved with increasing the superstructure's height by 10 cm. The sapper-version's problem could only be solved by relocating the personal equipment as follows:

1. the rifle, gas mask, breadbags stay with the soldier
2. the long handled tools would be fixed on the vehicle's outside

34 HL VKF 6312/eln.1.-1943. alapszám, 5112/eln.1.-1943. iktatószám
35 HL VKF 6312/eln.1.-1943.

3. the rucksacks, overcoats and blankets would be placed in boxes outside on the superstructure.

The demolition charges and technical equipment were also placed in holders, fixed besides the toolbox.

The members of the trial-group also requested a holder for a light machine gun on the front armour plate and to cut 2 openings both in the front and sidewalls to improve the visual conditions.[36]

The redesigned prototype was trialed again between 30th August – 4th September 1943 , and this time it was accepted in all aspects. The Institue of Military Technology recommended the authoratization of the 43M. LEHEL Á (árkász – sapper) and S (sebesültszállító – wounded) in the Royal Hungarian Army.[37]

According to the original plans, 9 LEHEL from the second batch of NIMRÓDs were to be taken out, and a further 28 vehicles were planned to be ordered as an extra besides the already ordered 89 self-propelled autocannons from MÁVAG.[38]

Finally, the General Staff decided to postpone the production of the LEHEL, and emphasized that the chassis will be needed for a long time for the NIMRÓDs.[39]

There is no further information on the fate of the LEHEL. It is unlikely that even damaged NIMRÓDs were rebuilt as armoured ambulance versions.

36 HL HM 31369/3ln.3.b.-1943. alapszám, 51155/eln.3.b.-1943. iktatószám, HM 58848/eln.3.b.-1943.
37 HL VKF 6312/eln.1.-1943.
38 HL HM 31369/3ln.3.b.-1943. alapszám, 30927/eln.3.b.-1943. iktatószám
39 HL VKF 6184/eln.1.-1943.

L-62 TANK-HUNTER	
Technical data	
Overall length	5320 mm
Overall width	2300 mm
Overall height	2560 mm
Ground clearance	350 mm
Track width	280 mm
Track gauge	2066 mm
Weight (operational condition w/ crew)	10500 kp
Ground pressure	-
Engine	
Manufacturer/type	Büssing-NAG Type L8V/36TR
Type	four-cycle
Cylinders	8
Bore and stroke	107/110
Engine capacity	7913 cm^3
Operating rpm	2700/min
Performance	155 HP
Deployment data	
Combat weight (Without crew and ammunition)	-
Max. Traction	7800 kp
Max. Speed	50 km/h
Range:	
Road	225 km
Cross-country	150 km
Climbing capacity	40°
Max. Cross slope	34°
Step	0,6 – 0,8 m
Trench crossing	2,0 – 2,2 m
Fording depth	0,8 m
Min. Turning radius	10 m
Pivot turning	-
Gears	I-V. + reverse
Fuel capacity	250 l
Fuel consumption:	
Road	100 liter/100 km
Cross-country	150 liter/100 km
Armour:	
Front	10-13 mm
Rear	7 mm
Side	10 mm
Roof	----
Bottom	6 mm
Armament	40 mm anti-aircraft cannon
Ammunition type	40 mm fragmentation 40 mm armour-piercing
Amount of ammunition	160 rounds
Rate of fire	-
Crew	1+4[40]

40M. NIMRÓD TANK-HUNTER AND ANTI-AIRCRAFT CANNON	
Technical data	
Overall length	5320 mm
Overall width	2300 mm
Overall height	2800 mm
Ground clearance	350 mm

40 VKF 3412/eln.1.-1940.; HM 13457/eln.3.b.-1940.

Track width		280 mm
Track gauge		2066 mm
Weight (operational condition w/crew)		ca. 11000 kp
Ground pressure		-
Engines		
	NIMRÓD I	NIMRÓD II
Manufacturer/type	Büssing NAG Type L8V/36TR	Ganz VIII VGT 107
Type	four-cycle	
Cylinders	8	8
Bore and stroke	107/110	107/110
Engine capacity	7913 cm^3	7913 cm^3
Operating rpm	2700/min.	2700/min.
Performance	155 HP	155 HP
Deployment datas		
Combat weight (without crew and ammo)		
Max. Traction		7800 kp
Max. Speed		50 km/h
Range:		
Road		225 km
Cross-country		150 km
Climbing capacity		40°
Max. Cross slope		34°
Step		0,6 – 0,8 m
Trench crossing		2,0 – 2,2 m
Fording depth		0,8 m
Min. Turning radius		10 m
Pivot turning		-
Gears		I – V + reverse

Fuel capacity	250 l
Fuel consumption:	
Road	100 liter/100 km
Cross-country	150 liter/100 km
Armour:	
Front	10-13 mm
Rear	7 mm
Side	10 mm
Roof	----
Bottom	6 mm
Armament	40 mm anti-aircraft cannon
Ammunition	40 mm 36 M. armor-piercing (AP) shell
	40 mm 39 M. high-explosive (HE) shell
	42a M. high-explosive anti-tank (HEAT) shell
Amount of ammunition	160 rounds
Rate of fire	120 / min
Crew	1+5[41]

ARMOURED PERSONNEL CARRIER ON NIMRÓD CHASSIS

Technical data	
Overall length	ca. 4900 mm
Overall width	2300 mm
Overall height	1850 mm
Ground clearance	350 mm
Track width	280 mm
Track gauge	2066 mm
Weight (operational condition w/ crew)	ca. 10500 kp
Ground pressure	0.50 kp/cm^2

41 VKF 3412/eln.1.-1940.; HM 13457/eln.3.b.-1940.; HM 566204/3.b.-1940

Engine	
Manufacturer/type	Büssing-NAG Type L8V/36TR
Type	four-stroke
Cylinders	8
Bore and stroke	107/110
Engine capacity	7913 cm^3
Operating speed	2700/min.
Performance	155 HP
Deployment data	
Combat weight (Without crew and ammo)	8340 kp
Max. Traction	7800 kp
Max. Speed	50 km/h
Range:	
Road	225 km
Cross-country	150 km
Climbing capacity	40°
Max. Cross slope	27°
Step	0,6 – 0,8 m
Trench crossing	2,0 – 2,2 m
Fording depth	0,8 m
Min. Turning radius	10 m
Pivot turning	-
Gears	I – V + reverse
Fuel capacity	250 l
Fuel consumption:	
Road	100 liter/100 km
Cross-country	150 liter/100 km
Armour:	
Front	10-13 mm
Rear	7 mm
Side	10 mm
Roof	----
Bottom	6 mm
Armament	-
Crew	1+11

43M. Lehel armoured amboulance and personnel carrier

Technical data	
Overall length	ca. 4900 mm
Overall width	2300 mm
Overall height	2800 mm
Ground clearance	350 mm
Track width	280 mm
Track gauge	2066 mm
Weight (operational condition w/crew)	ca. 11000 kp
Ground pressure	-

Engines	PROTOTYPE	PLANNED SERIES
Manufacturer/type	Büssing-NAG Type L8V/36TR	Ganz VIII VGT 107
Type	four-cycle	four-cycle
Cylinders	8	8
Bore and stroke	107/110	107/110
Engine capacity	7913 cm^3	7913 cm^3
Operating rpm	2700/min.	2700/min.
Performance	155 HP	155 HP

Deployment data	
Combat weight (Without crew and ammo)	8340 kp
Max. Traction	7800 kp
Max. Speed	50 km/h
Range:	
Road	225 km
Cross-country	150 km
Climbing capacity	40°
Max. Cross slope	27°
Step	0,6 – 0,8 m
Trench crossing	2,0 – 2,2 m
Fording depth	0,8 m
Min. Turning radius	10 m
Pivot turning	-
Gears	I – V + reverse
Fuel capacity	250 l

Fuel consumption:		
Road		100 liter/100 km
Cross-country		150 liter/100 km
Armour:		
Front		10-13 mm
Rear		7 mm
Side		10 mm
Roof		-
Bottom		6 mm
Armament		1x8 mm 31M. light machine gun
		2x9 mm 39M. submachine gun
Ammount of ammunition		1500 rounds (light MG)
		560 round submachine gun
Crew	LEHEL ‚Á'	LEHEL ‚S'
	1+8	1+4+4

Attila Bonhardt via Ferenc Kovács

L-62 tank-hunter, produced by the Swedish company A.B. Landswerk (Landskrona). This fighting vehicle is a 40mm Bofors anti-aircraft autocannon built on the chassis of an L-60 light tank. The autocannon was designed for air-defense and anti-tank roles. Inside the welded superstructure the fighting compartment was placed between the driver's compartment (front) and the engine bay (rear). The 360° rotating, open-topped, conical turret had space for the autocannon and 4 man crew.

Attila Bonhardt via Ferenc Kovács

Front right view of the L-62. Clearly seen is the modern, angled silhouette of the hull and the conical shaped turret. The sloped armour reduced the angle of the impact, which is why the designers settled for 6-13 mm thick armour. On the rear end of the right mudguard, which was bolted to the superstructure, a square toolbox can be seen.

Front view of the L-62, with its gun raised to air-defense position. The horizontal and vertical optical sights are visible on both sides of the gun. The gun barrel could be lifted via the slit cut into the front plate of the turret. When the gun was in a raised position nothing protected this slit so a shell had free access into the turret. As well, the two openings for the optical sights were unprotected which endangered the sights and also the battle readiness of the L-62. On the front of the hull the driver's cupola can be seen.

Attila Bonhardt via Ferenc Kovács

L-62 with its turret in 7 o'clock position and lowered gun. The man in the turret illustrates well how tight the compartment was for a four-man crew. The picture clearly shows the up-to-date running gear with torsion bars, which made it possible to move the wheels independently from each other in a vertical direction. All in all, the experts found the L-62 suitable for authorization in the Royal Hungarian Army with minor changes.

Gk. ismeretek, 40 M. 'Nimród' hk. vadász és lgv.gá.

Left side view of the fighting vehicle with Hungarian modifications, which were put into service in the Royal Hungarian Army as 40M. 'NIMRÓD' tank-hunter and anti-aircraft cannon. The most important of these changes were the lengthening of the original cone-shaped turret and the increasing of the front part's height. Plates, so-called 'gapings', were fastened to both sides of the gun barrel's opening with springs which closed automatically such that the smallest possible gap was left at every position of the barrel.

Gk. ismeretek, 40 M. 'Nimród' hk. vadász és lgv.gá.

Right side view of the NIMRÓD. The up-to-date torsion bar suspension had five rubber-tired double roadwheels on each side, with steel idler wheels, which adjusted the track tension. The tracks consisted of 132 links on each side and were driven by the front sprocket wheels. Each track link has a guide tooth in the middle, which prevented the tracks from falling off. These teeth ran in between the double roadwheels. Three return rollers prevented extreme sagging of the tracks. Note the Hungarian-made tool-boxes on the back part of the mudguard, which were narrower and longer then the original ones.

Front view of the NIMRÓD. The tightly closed 'gapings' and the Hungarian-designed armoured plates of the horizontal and vertical aiming devices can be clearly seen. The plates were moved together with the devices. The covering plates completely closed the openings of the aiming devices when the gun was in a horizontal position. These openings were much wider on the Hungarian vehicle than on the original Swedish version. The asymmetrical shape of the turret is also visible. The right-side optic's opening (left to the viewer) for the horizontal sight is smaller and has a different shape than the vertical sight.

Gk. ismeretek, 40 M. 'Nimród' hk. vadász és lgv.gá.

Rear view of the NIMRÓD shows the vertical armour plate of the turret's rear and the engine deck. The dark square in the middle of the turret is the opening for the cartridge case-ejector where the empty cases were discarded out of the turret. The fuel filler opening's cover is on the left side of the engine deck. The two circular plates covered the air-intakes. These were placed asymmetrically because the engine was slightly shifted to the right. Between the engine deck cover and the rear armour plate the ventilation grille can be seen. The silencer of the exhaust and its pipes are on the rear plate. Also, the towing hooks and the locks of the toolboxes are clearly seen in this sharp picture.

Gk. ismeretek, 40 M. 'Nimród' hk. vadász és lgv.gá.

This plan view of the NIMRÓD shows the horseshoe-shaped new turret which was designed in Hungary. The four crew seats are also visible. The range-operator (1st operator) sits on the right side of the gun-breech, the horizontal-gunner (2nd operator) sits in front of him, the vertical-gunner (4th operator) sits on the left front, while the loader (3rd operator) sits behind him. The commander had his place in the lengthened rear in the right corner. The R-5a radio was placed in the left rear corner but in this case it's not installed yet. The double handles of the aiming devices are clearly seen. These were covered with rubber and one of them could lift up the barrel to 90° within ca. 10 seconds, while the other rotated the turret 360° within ca. 20 seconds.

Attila Bonhardt

According to the square-shaped toolboxes and the H-400 license plate, this is the prototype of the domestically designed turret on the original L-62 chassis (although it's not correct as the L-62 was originally issued with H-004). The picture clearly shows the cover plates of the optical sights and the shape of the turret. The cover plates which closed the openings of the aiming devices had two steel bands (the so-called 'splash covers') on both sides to protect the openings against splinters. We also have a good view of the gun-breech, the feeding mechanism, the ejector and the seats for the four-man crew. The driver's cupola is turned to the right and shows the very tight hatch.

Attila Bonhardt

Rear view of the same vehicle from above. This rare picture shows the inner side of the turret's front: the springs of the 'gapings' and the backside of the aiming devices' cover plates. Also, a clear view of the horizontal and vertical sight's optical viewers and its tube holders. These tubes also transmitted the data. In front of the vertical sight we can see the driver's compartment. The driver could sneak into the turret in an emergency situation.

Attila Bonhardt via Zoltán Barczi

Experimental aiming device in front of the vertical-gunner's seat. It was designed at the request of tank officers, who found it too difficult to handle the double (horizontal and vertical) aiming device. Eventually, it wasn't authorized, because it was inadequate for the air-defense role – which was the NIMRÓD's primary mission. There are empty holders for the four-shell magazines on the inner side of the turret's wall.

Attila Bonhardt via Huba Csethe

The driver sits on the left side between the front armour and the turret. He was protected with an armoured cupola, which was completely rotatable so that he could get in or out of the vehicle. This picture demonstrates well the tightness of the hatch. The driver laughs and shows the steering wheel, which was simply removable by pulling a pin. Without removing the steering wheel it was almost impossible to get in or out of the NIMRÓD. The turret ring and the lower part of the left 'gapings' can be seen directly behind the driver's head. To the left we can see the pivot of the protective cupola.

Attila Bonhardt via Jenő Zálnoky

The driver's place from a distance. The armoured cupola is turned to the right. On the driver's left side, we can see the marker light on the mudguard, protected with a metal cover. The bolted front armour covered the steering mechanism and the transmission. The headlight was placed in the middle of the front plate and protected by an armoured cover. The grill of the headlight could be opened from the driver's seat. Below the headlight we can see the small oval emblem of the manufacturer: top line – MÁVAG; bottom line – BUDAPEST-DIÓSGYŐR. Between them was the licence plate number of the vehicle.

Removing the front plate to have access to the transmission and the steering mechanism. We can see part of the steering mechanism under the partly removed plate. Tools are laying in front of the driver's hatch.

Fortepan

NIMRÓD H-064 examined by factory workers during a test drive, probably on the training ground of Hajmáskér. In the background we can see a crane which was used to lift the engines of the tanks. The curved cover plate ('splash-cover') beside the horizontal aiming device which protected it against fragments can be clearly seen. There was also a small horizontal plate underneath. The driver's cupola is in the open position (so we can see its left side) and shows the latches. The small plate on the left side of the cupola covered a slit used when driving with a closed cupola. It was openable from the inside.

The same vehicle from the other side. We can compare the protection of the horizontal and vertical aiming devices. The opening for the vertical sight (left) is wider, no 'splash cover' and no lower horizontal plate. The commanders usually didn't wear earphones integrated into the helmet, but instead wore them on or under their cap.

These trials included long range drives too, fulfilled by factory workers in the presence of the members of the Military Acceptance Committee (Katonai Átvételi Bizottság – KÁB). The NIMRÓDs – covered with tarpaulins – are waiting for the move. The flash suppressor is also covered with a cap. Employees of MÁVAG are standing around. We can clearly see the driver's closed cupola and the visors with armoured, splinter-safe glass, and the front vision slit covered with a movable armoured cover plate. We can see the pivot of the cupola on the right side of it.

Presentation of NIMRÓDs that have just been handed over by the Army in April 1942, Hajmáskér.

Attila Bonhardt via Emil Galánthay

Attila Bonhardt via László Tóth

The first NIMRÓDs were received by the Royal Hungarian 51. Anti-Tank Battalion accommodated in Budapest. The crew of H-068 stand next to the vehicle before getting the order 'Boarding!'. The commander (Lieutenant György Káplán) stands on the right side of the NIMRÓD, behind him are the 1st gunner and then the 2nd gunner. The driver is already in his seat (he would stand in front on the left side, where now we can see the loader). The 4th operator stands behind the vehicle's left side. To get in the NIMRÓD, the crew had to climb up on the engine deck and get into the vehicle through the rear wall of the turret.

The same vehicle on the training ground behind the Franz Joseph Infantry barracks (Budapest, Üllői út). The NIMRÓD drives into a temporary firing emplacement. We can see how cramped the turret was even after it was enlarged. The gun barrel is lowered, the covers of the aiming devices and the driver's cupola are in closed positions.

The same vehicle in firing position, with its gun barrel elevated into air-defense position. The sprung cover plates completely closed the slit on the turret's front. The protective shields of the aiming devices move along with the gun, exposing the openings. In the background we can see another NIMRÓD.

H-68 moves out of the firing emplacement. The gun is in a lowered position again and the protecting plates are covering every opening now. The crew members are standing in their places so they exposed themselves. During action they sit on their seats and are covered by the turret armour which protects against splinters.

Attila Bonhardt via Dezső Legány

The crew of H-075 NIMRÓD practising to fight against close assaults. Although the equipment requirements specified only one submachine gun for a NIMRÓD, all the crew members hold German MP 40s in their hands. We can see again the ‘splash cover’ on the right side of the turret’s front.

Attila Bonhardt via Ferenc Kovács

The double rubber-tired roadwheels of the NIMRÓD. Clearly seen is the crank between the first and second wheels. The crank was connected to a rod spring which allowed the wheels to move independently from each other in a vertical direction. We can see how the track guides fit into the gap between the double roadwheels. Even the pins of the track links are clearly seen in this picture (each track consisted of 132 links).

Attila Bonhardt via László Tóth

Front view of the NIMRÓD. The 1941M. insignia was painted on the front armour – every driver's nightmare -as the red-white-green cross made a perfect target for the anti-tank gunners. We can see the headlight's armoured grill in the middle of the front armour and the fan of the transmission on the right side. The latter was also covered with an armoured grill.

The driver's cupola in open position. The drivers drove like this during march for a better view. The driver's seat could be levelled up and down with a handle – in this case we can see it in the lowest position. The left position light and the cover plate of the vertical aiming device can be seen clearly once again.

Attila Bonhardt via Zsolt Pálinkás

Similar view, but this time the driver's seat is in an elevated position which allowed a better view. We can see the inner side of the cupola and the bolted front armour with the headlight and the grill of the fan. We can also observe the angle of the turret's wall which decreased the penetration angle and thus increased the protection.

Attila Bonhardt

Vehicles of an armoured unit. There are TOLDI light tanks in front of the NIMRÓDs. The former's chassis was the basis of the anti-aircraft autocannon which became the NIMRÓD. We can observe the similarity of the running gear, which was different only in the size and the number of roadwheels. The tankers wear armoured crew headgear, while the crew of the autocannons (except the driver) wear helmets.

Attila Bonhardt via Zoltán Babucs

The crew of a NIMRÓD posing in front of their vehicle. The gun barrel is in an elevated position. The lower part of the two-piece sprung covers is in the closed position and we can see the open bay for the barrel. The springs completely pull the plates against the barrel, leaving only a small gap between the cover plates. The driver holds the steering wheel in his hands.

Attila Bonhardt via János Hunyad

The maintenance was a daily routine for the crews. The soldiers of the II./Tank Regiment 1's (Jászberény) autocannon company are maintaining their vehicles in front of the garages. They wear the same two-piece grey canvas suit that the tankers did – which could even be worn over their uniform. We can see the regular stowage on the left side. There are tie-down brackets on the side of the superstructure.

Attila Bonhardt via János Hunyad

The same vehicles from the other side. We can see the regular stowage of the right side on the rear vehicle: the toolbox and the jack. The shovel was secured on the right side of the engine deck.

Attila Bonhardt via Iván Martsa

A company of the 51. Anti-Tank Battalion march back from the training ground, spring 1942. We can observe the cover plates of the horizontal aiming device and the gun's opening. Also, the handles of the driver's cupola are clearly seen on the inner side of it.

Attila Bonhardt via Sándor Zágony

To save the vehicles, the tanks were transported by rail to the firing range. Here we can see the NIMRÓDs of the Tank Battalion of Jászberény, loaded onto a train. The open-topped vehicles are covered with camouflaged tarpaulins to protect against the weather.

Attila Bonhardt via Sándor Zágony

Commanders practising the radio on a training ground in the shadow of NIMRÓD H-059. Cadet Sergeant Sándor Zágony is standing in the middle. We can see the ‘splash cover’ and the horizontal plate protecting the horizontal aiming device. Also, we have a good view of the handles on the inner side of the driver’s opened cupola.

Fortepan

Common training of NIMRÓDs and 36M. 40 mm Bofors anti-aircraft autocannons. We can see air-defense instruments around the battle-ready towed anti-aircraft autocannon: Gamma – Juhász 36M. direction-finder and speed meter, and 1,25m range-finder. The gun barrels are in 45° position, but the crew is absent so there is probably no sign of the target plane yet.

A NIMRÓD on live-fire training. In the foreground is a crewman with the 1,25m range-finder authorized for the anti-tank and air-defense autocannon platoons. The vehicle's gun is raised to 45°. We can see the cover plates of the aiming devices above the turret's edge. These moved together with the gun barrel. The loader watches the sky with his naked eye, while the commander uses his binoculars. The rest of the crew are waiting for the order in their positions, so we can't see them.

Fortepan

A company of 51. Anti-Tank Battalion practising the air-defense of a column on the road to the training ground near Zsámbék, spring 1942. The cover plates of the aiming devices are clearly seen in this picture. The crews are not in place, so the picture was probably taken during a break.

The same coloumn at Zsámbék. In the background we can see the ruins of the Romanesque style Premontre monastery church.

Attila Bonhardt via Sándor Zágony

The students of the Teacher Training School of Zsámbék offer some food to the soldiers. Cadet Sergeant Sándor Zágony is standing in the middle of the group in front of a NIMRÓD with raised gun.

A NIMRÓD of the 51. Anti-Tank Battalion at Zsámbék, spring 1942. The vehicle was probably decorated for the National Holiday of 15th March (Hungarian Revolution of 1848). The soldier in leather coat leaning against the mudguard is Cadet Sergeant Ferenc Nagy, the commander of the vehicle.

Attila Bonhardt via Family Gergelyffy

There was strict order to clean the vehicles after they returned from training. Soldiers of the 51. Anti-Tank Battalion prepare for this in the yard of Franz Joseph barracks. The gun barrel is in the lowest -5° positon so we can take a look inside the flash suppressor. Besides the details of the front part of the vehicle we can also see the rarely seen two small towing hooks bolted onto the lower part of the front armour. First Lieutenant János Gergelyffy, the commander of the 2. Company, is standing next to the vehicle – he was killed in action on the Eastern Front at the River Don.

The external wash had to be done with water jet. The soldiers pay extra attention to the running gear to remove mud, stuck stones and other objects. The tarpaulin of the left toolbox was removed before cleaning. We can see the holders of the tarpaulin's straps above the toolbox. The field kitchen is also waiting for cleaning.

The 51. Anti-Tank Battalion was subordinated to the Royal Hungarian 1. Armoured Division in the spring of 1942, when the unit was sent to the River Don. Governor Miklós Horthy inspected the units of the division on the training ground at Esztergom-tábor. This is one of the battalion's companies lined up for the inspection. The column is led by a Toldi of the company commander and it is followed by the NIMRÓDs.

Attila Bonhardt via Pál Illés

The same column from the other side. The crews are standing in place and waiting for the Governor to arrive. We can see the olive green – wood brown – sand yellow camouflage of the tank-hunters.

Attila Bonhardt via József Basó

NIMRÓD H-070 during the Governor's inspection at Esztergom-tábor, May 1942. The conspicuous insignia authorized in 1941 was painted on the turret's side and on the front plate. The front license number was painted on a distinct white base. Next to the tank-hunter we can see the dark grey T-38 tanks of the division's 30. Tank Regiment handed over by the Germans. In the background stands the Mount Strázsa.

Attila Bonhardt via László Posch

One of the companies of the 51. Anti-Tank Battalion at Esztergom-tábor, 1st June 1942. The NIMRÓDs still have camouflage paint, but all of their insignias have been removed. In the background we can see the company commander's TOLDI tank and an Opel Blitz truck loaded with jerry cans.

NIMRÓDs marching to the Don. We can see the emblem of the 51. Anti-Tank Battalion on the rear wall of the NIMRÓD: a horse riding archer aiming upward. The vehicle has the new insignia which was introduced in 1942: a white cross on black background. The crew's gear is hanging outside of the turret. The NIMRÓD is passing by a camouflaged BOTOND cross-country truck. At the crossroads there is another NIMRÓD with the new insignia, following a Pz. IV F1 of the 30. Tank Regiment.

Attila Bonhardt via János Szollár

The units of the 1. Field Armoured Division were sent back and forth during the battles of the Korotojak and Uriv bridgeheads in August 1942. A camouflaged NIMRÓD runs through a poor Soviet village at full throttle. The crew is wearing rolled-up sleeves because of the heat.

Attila Bonhardt via Iván Csányi

A grain-camouflaged NIMRÓD of 51. Anti-Tank Battalion crosses a Russian settlement on the Don Front in August 1942. The crew wears goggles to protect against the dust, stirred up by the vehicles.

A NIMRÓD with foliage stands at the banks of the Don. There is a 1,25m range-finder in the ditch. The soldier – just like the vehicle's crew – is watching the sky to spot the enemy's planes on the other side. The 25 cm long flash suppressor is clearly seen at the end of the barrel. Its function was to hide the muzzle flash of the gun bursts.

A NIMRÓD tank-hunter and armoured anti-aircraft autocannon in firing emplacement at the Don. The crew is watching the sky, the driver is ready to start. We can see the bolted front armour plate with the grill cover of the headlight and the fan of the transmission and steering mechanism.

Attila Bonhardt via Family Gergelyffy

The crew of this NIMRÓD spends their free time cleaning and repairing their clothes in the middle of an unharvested cornfield. While part of the crew take care of their equipment, the others are watching. The NIMRÓD is camouflaged with grains. We can see the new insignia on the plain green vehicle introduced in 1942 and the white indicator which helped the drivers during march. There are a few jerry cans on the mudguard's front section.

Attila Bonhardt via Béla Ringelhann

Poorly camouflaged NIMRÓD of the 51. Anti-Tank Battalion, during the third Uriv-battle, September 1942. The autocannon's barrel is in 45° position and the commander is watching the sky with his binoculars. Nevertheless, the crewmembers are posing with their submachine guns since they are not in action. The presence of the farmers also confirms this theory. In any case the vehicle is combat-ready with jerry cans jammed behind the jack.

Attila Bonhardt via László Posch

A Hungarian tank-hunter after the bridgehead battles of the summer in a destroyed Russian village, September 1942. The crewmembers' equipment (gas masks, helmets, breadbags) are hanging on the turret's side. We can see the unit sign of the 51. Anti-Tank Battalion, a horse riding archer, aiming upward in a white parallelogram behind the officer's shoulder, who wears the so-called Birgeli boots.

Attila Bonhardt via Zoltán Barczi

While the 51. Anti-Tank Battalion fought on the Eastern Front, the training of the autocannon units and their equipping continued at home. Here new recruits are getting familiar with a NIMRÓD with the new insignia, fall 1942.

NIMRÓD H-088 of the 51. Armoured Autocannon Battalion's (the renamed 51. Anti-Tank Battalion) replacement unit with new insignia and black licence number painted on the base colour. This vehicle was used for training. Here we can see how it looked when the driver worked with a closed cupola. There are three periscopes just beneath the edge of the cupola on the front and both sides. In case these were damaged, the driver could use the three armoured glass visors, protected by small movable armoured plates.

Attila Bonhardt via Iván Martsa

Interesting shot of two NIMRÓDs, belonging to the II./ Tank Battalion 1's autocannon company. The closer vehicle has the old national insignia and the white-based licence plate, while the other one doesn't have insignia, and has its licence numbers painted on the camouflage colours. The first vehicle's engine deck is open so we can see the edge of the aerial identification insignia and the lock of the engine deck on the right side. The gun barrel of the other vehicle is lowered down to -5°, so the sprung plates can't close perfectly.

Fortepan

The handover of the second batch of 89 NIMRÓD began in April 1943. They received licence numbers between 1H-630 and 1H-718. Two brand new, camouflaged armoured anti-aircraft autocannons (1H-642 and 1H-643) are waiting in the Royal Hungarian Army's Vehicle Depot to be handed over to the troops. We can see how the guide teeth fit into the gap between the roadwheels and the return rollers. Note the position of periscopes and the armoured cover plates of the vision slits on the right side and front of the driver's cupola.

Attila Bonhardt via Zoltán Barci

This rare picture shows how the crew of a NIMRÓD had to leave the vehicle. They had to step over the rear wall of the turret then jump off from the engine deck. When mounting the vehicle they also had to use the engine deck. While the gun barrel is in a slightly raised position, the sprung cover plates don't close perfectly. The gun barrel would sit tight in the small bulges of the cover plates at 0°.

Attila Bonhardt via László Vécsey

A rare view again, this time from the position of the loader. The inner side of the turret's front armour and the spring of the left cover plate are clearly seen. The holder for the four-shell rack on the right side is empty. The cover plates of the aiming devices were bolted to a rod which was fixed to the gun barrel. In this way the cover plates moved along with the devices.

Attila Bonhardt via József Riegler

This NIMRÓD looks abandoned on a training ground in the spring of 1943. However, if we take a closer look we can see the crew, taking a break under the bushes.

Attila Bonhardt via Zsolt Pálinkás

The same vehicle from the other side. This photograph clearly shows the exhaust pipes and the positon of the large rear towing hook. The shell ejector was in the middle of the turret's vertical rear plate, the R-5a radio was installed on the left next to it. The handles above the shovel were to help the crew getting onto the NIMRÓD.

The left rear of the same vehicle. The Non-Commissioned Officer School's emblem (the Kinizsi-shield: a sword holding right arm) can be seen on the left side of the rear plate. Unfortunately the licence number on the other side is illegible, but we have a good view of the track tension bar at the inner side of the right idler wheel, the silencer and the left pipe of the exhaust. There are two handles above the left toolbox (on which there is a folded tarpaulin) which helped the crew climb onto the NIMRÓD.

The crew of NIMRÓD 300 posing in front of their vehicle after a successful firing practise. They wear two-piece overalls which were worn by mechanics. In the middle of the group we can see the instructor, a Sergeant. The radio was installed on rails in the left rear corner of the turret. Note the base of the rod antenna.

Attila Bonhardt via Iván Martsa

NIMRÓD 1H-634 of II./ Tank-Regiment 1 (Jászberény) during a break in the live firing exercise. Private First Class Iván Martsa sits in the driver's seat. The commander is wearing earphones, he may be listening to some music. All the details of the front plate and the turret's right side can be seen.

Attila Bonhardt via Iván Martsa

The same vehicle with its turret at 10 o'clock position, with slightly raised gun barrel.

Close front-view of the NIMRÓD which clearly shows the details of the front plate, the grill armour of the headlight and the fan, the bolts, the lower part of the front plate and the small towing hooks. Note how the teeth of the sprocket wheel fit into the track links. But the driver's cupola is the most interesting: we have a very good view of the periscopes and the small pads above them. These small pads protected the head of the driver when he drove with a closed cupola.

Preparing to celebrate the Day of Saint Christopher, the Patron Saint of the travellers in the yard of the Royal Hungarian Army's depot, Mátyásföld, 27th July 1943. Two beautifully rebuilt NIMRÓD were the decoration. According to the white kill rings on the gun barrels, these vehicles belonged to the 51. Anti-Tank Battalion, which returned from the Eastern Front during the fall of 1942. In front of the vehicles there are two captured T-34 engines used for instruction.

Day of Saint Christopher, the Patron Saint of the travellers in the yard of the Royal Hungarian Army's depot, Mátyásföld, 27th July 1943. According to the license number, NIMRÓD H-071 was transported home from the Eastern Front for factory overhaul. During the repair work both vehicles received camouflage paint and new insignias (white cross in black square). The large one on the engine deck of the NIMRÓD on the left served as aerial recognition.

Attila Bonhardt via Lajos Harmath

Parade of the Ludovika Military Academy's tank company in front of newly inaugurated Lieutenants on the Nagyrét (Large Field) behind the Academy, 20th August 1943. The company's NIMRÓD is just passing the tribune. There is a TURÁN medium tank in front of the NIMRÓD, which is followed by TOLDI light tanks.

Attila Bonhardt via Zoltán Tóth

Filling up the NIMRÓD with fuel. The clamping screw besides the soldier’s foot was to close the engine deck . The armoured fan of the ventilator was placed between the engine deck and the rear plate.

Attila Bonhardt via Zoltán Tóth

Practising the radio, 52. Anti-aircraft Autocannon Battalion, Cegléd. We can see the handles above the toolbox on the left side which helped the crew get onto the vehicle. Note the track tension bar on the inner side of the right idler wheel.

A NIMRÓD of II./ Tank-Regiment 1 (Jászberény) took part in a parade on a local sports field. We can see five kill rings on the 'saluting' gun barrel. According to this, this is the third rebuilt NIMRÓD of the 51. Anti-Tank Battalion which was brought back as a damaged vehicle from the Eastern Front.

Parade march of II./ Tank-Regiment 1, during the farewell ceremony of 102. Independent Tank Company, 6th December 1943. We can see the armoured autocannon platoon of the company. The NIMRÓDs are saluting with their raised gun barrels, the crews are standing in tight watch in front of the dignitaries. The drivers wear tanker's helmets with integrated earphones, while the crews wear ordinary helmets.

Attila Bonhardt via János Szollár

MÁVAG handed over the NIMRÓDs with plain olive green paint from the fall of 1943 onward. These vehicles take a break in a village during the trials of KÁB (Katonai Átvevő Bizottság – Military Receiving Committee). The officer is accredited by the KÁB, the civilians are representatives and leaders of the factory. For some unknown reason the gun barrel of the first vehicle is in the raised position which was uncommon during a march.

Attila Bonhardt via János Szollár

The same place, a little bit later. The turret of the first NIMRÓD is turned to the 9 o'clock position. Note the plain colour of the vehicle.

Attila Bonhardt via Pál Illés

A NIMRÓD of the 51. Armoured Autocannon Battalion at Zsámbék. Note how the roadwheels follow the undulations of the ground. The driver (standing in his hatch) wears his 35M. tanker uniform according to the rules – his leather jacket is tucked into his pants. The officer leaning against the front plate wears only the jacket of the uniform. The rest of the crew wear cloth coats.

Attila Bonhardt via Béla Todorovics

A NIMRÓD of the 3. Motorized Rifle Battalion (Aszód) takes a break during driving practice. As usual, the gun barrel is covered with a protective cap. The soldiers wear two-piece overalls. Lieutenant János Szeder is sitting on the opened cupola of the driver. He wears a simple shirt and riding boots. In front of the insignia we can see the General Military Vehicle Emblem: the coat of arms of Hungary surrounded by a wreath laid on a crossed gun barrel, a rifle, a sword and a helmet. The base of the emblem is gold and the coat of arms is colourful. The sticker format emblem was placed beneath the turret in the middle of the superstructure.

This NIMRÓD also took a break in front of a rural mansion during a road march. There is a barrel in the turret. The Hungarian fighting vehicles often carried reserve fuel (especially in operational areas), but usually on the engine deck. According to the rules, the barrels immediately had to be thrown away before a firefight. The officer leaning against the vehicle wears some home-made overalls, while the corporal next to him has a summer uniform.

Fortepan

Front left view of the same vehicle. This is a rare picture of the opened armoured grill of the headlight, so we have a clear view of it. The gun barrel is in prescribed position, with protective cap on the flash suppressor.

A NIMRÓD of the Military Academy's Tank Company in Zsámbék, June 1944. The company was evacuated from Budapest because of the Anglo-Saxon bombing raids. The camouflaged vehicle stands beside a wall. Unfortunately only the white band of the shield can be seen from the licence number. The meaning of the white circle painted on the right front part of the driver's cupola is unknown.

A well camouflaged NIMRÓD of the Military Academy (covered with tarpaulin) hiding under a tree at Zsámbék. It is impossible to determine if it has camouflage paint or plain green colour. At least the tarpaulin is the authorized camouflaged version.

Attila Bonhardt via László Vécsey

The Tank Company of the Royal Hungarian Army ‘Csaba királyfi’ Fast Troops Cadet School in Marosvásárhely, 4th June 1944 during the school’s flag inauguration ceremony. We can see two olive green NIMRÓDs on the right side, next to them there are three olive green 40M. TURÁN medium tanks. The front and rear mudguards of the vehicles were painted white for the ceremony. The crews are standing easy next to their vehicles and waiting for the beginning of the ceremony. Despite the warm weather of June, the cadets wear 35M. leather tanker uniforms and cloth field caps.

Attila Bonhardt via Béla Todorovics

NIMRÓD of the 3. Motorized Rifle Battalion's armoured autocannon company on the training ground behind the garages, summer 1944. The vehicle's gun barrel is raised to 90°. Two soldiers are posing on the protective cover plates of the aiming devices which moved along with the gun. We can see how the 'gapings' completely closed the opening of the gun barrel and the uncovered large openings of the aiming devices.

Attila Bonhardt via Zoltán Barczi

A NIMRÓD of 52. Armoured Anti-Aircraft Autocannon Battalion crossing a river in Galicia. The temporary bridge was built on the river, probably the Bistrica. The driver is focusing on the logs, the crew hold the edge of the turret, and the sappers are just watching the movement. The crew's equipment is hanging on the turret with some bushes which serve as camouflage.

The 52. Armoured Anti-Aircraft Autocannon Battalion moves ahead in a destroyed Galician village after the successful river-crossing. Note the crew's equipment: the mess kits on the folded blanket and the 42M. gas mask canisters. Unfortunately only the first two digits (91) of the tactical number can be seen – the third one is covered by the soldier's leg. Most probably this is NIMRÓD '911' – the first vehicle of the 52. Armoured Anti-Aircraft Autocannon Battalion's 1st company. This is proved by the white bar seen on the left upper corner of the rear plate and the company commander's TOLDI, which has turret number '910'.

A NIMRÓD after a march on muddy roads. In this case it is better to drive with a closed cupola! We can see the front periscope and the visor slit underneath, between the legs of the two soldiers. Note the flash suppressor.

Attila Bonhardt via Péter Mujzer

Two NIMRÓDs camouflaged with pine branches. According to the turret numbers – ‘2023’ and ‘2022’ – these vehicles belonged to II./ Tank-Battalion 3’s autocannon company. Decoding the numbers: ‘2’ = II. battalion; ‘0’ = Staff; ‘2’ = autocannon company; ‘3’ = third vehicle of the company. The vehicles stand stepwise in a distance from each other, the gun barrels are in 45° position. Down in the valley we can see a TURÁN tank. Note the radio with the rod antenna in the turret and the General Military Vehicle Emblem in the middle of the superstructure on the nearest vehicle.

Attila Bonhardt via Péter Mujzer

Front left view of the same vehicle. It seems that the crew don't fear any attack as only one soldier is standing in the turret – the rest of the crew are sleeping on the ground. Their helmets are covered with mud to avoid the gleam of the glossy paint.

Attila Bonhardt via Pál Petró

Camouflaged NIMRÓD of III./ Tank-Regiment 3's autocannon company providing air protection at the edge of a Galician village, probably full of Hungarian troops. The vehicle's licence number is 1H-663. The gun barrel is in raised position, the 'gaping' completely closing the opening. The company commander Lieutenant Pál Petró is standing on the right side in the turret.

Attila Bonhardt via László Bombay

A NIMRÓD stands guard at the edge of a forest. The gun barrel is raised near to 90° position. The ‘gapings’ completely closed the opening of the gun barrel, but because of this, the openings of the aiming devices are uncovered. The sun shines on the periscope of the driver’s cupola. Note the cover plate of the driver’s visor slits. We can’t see any of the crew. The picture was probably taken during training.

While the NIMRÓDs of the 2. Armoured Division fought on the Eastern Front, the remaining autocannon units – mostly the 51. Armoured Autocannon Battalion – were used against the air raids in Hungary which began in April 1944. The 40 mm autocannons were used primarily against low flying attacking planes. This picture shows a NIMRÓD covered with camouflaged tarpaulin in a dug in position at the edge of a ploughed field. The superstitious crew have attached a horseshoe to the grill of the headlight. Somebody peacefully plows in the background.

Attila Bonhardt via Attila Vaspöri

This picture also shows a dug in NIMRÓD. Although the gun barrel fiercely stares at the sky, there's no crew members in the vehicle. Only a young girl takes the opportunity to take a commemorative photograph. Maybe the trees were to camouflage the NIMRÓD. We can see the large air recognition insignia and the grilled cover of the fan on the engine deck.

Attila Bonhardt via Huba Csethe

An autocannon of the 51. Armoured Autocannon Battalion in a permanent, well fortified position at Juta-domb (Juta-hill), Pesterzsébet. The gun barrel is in standby position, raised to 45°. We can see the ammo shells' end tips in the racks on the inner side of the turret's wall. Note the cover plates of the aiming devices on the turret's front, and the radio installed in the rear.

Attila Bonhardt via Dezső Legány

Rear view of the same gun emplacement and the same vehicle. Note the still empty ammo loading structure at the end of the gun breech and the tube system which fixed the cover plates of the aiming devices to the gun. This made it possible for it to move along with the gun barrel.

This picture was taken in the summer of 1945 and shows a badly damaged and looted NIMRÓD in a ditch somewhere in the former ‘Szentes-bridgehead’. The vehicle belonged to the 1. (reserve) Armoured Division. During the retreat in September 1944, the division’s vehicles were ordered to support the infantry one by one. The incompetent commanders used the NIMRÓDs for such tasks to which they were unfit because of their open-topped turret, armour and armament. This led to serious losses. Most probably this vehicle was lost due to a similar order.

TsAMO

This plain green NIMRÓD looks intact. The picture was taken in a trophy exhibition next to the river Moscow. The curious guests can get information about the vehicle from the data plate put on the front plate. Next to the NIMRÓD we can see a German Sd.Kfz. 7/2 half-track with 37 mm Flak 43 autocannon. Behind the German vehicle there is a Hungarian Zrínyi assault howitzer.

Attila Bonhardt

There is also a 'survivor' in Budapest, not only in Kubinka (Russia). This vehicle was unable to move, but was relatively intact when it survived the war in the yard of the Military Museum (the former 'Nándor' barracks). Somehow it also survived those years which were dangerous for 'fascist' weapons in the Eastern Block. The picture shows the NIMRÓD in the yard of the Military Museum, during the '60s. The main body and the turret is intact, the grill of the transmission's fan and the service panel under the headlight was removed but kept in storage. According to the small oval emblem next to the service panel, the license number of this vehicle was 1H-631.

Mátyás Pánczél

A rebuilt and (in theory) functional NIMRÓD in front of the Military Museum, 2013. Unfortunately the cover plates of the aiming devices weren't replaced during restoration, nor was the small oval emblem. In spite of this we can say that this is the best condition 40M. NIMRÓD armoured autocannon in the world.

Attila Bonhardt via Iván Martsa

The prototype of the LEHEL armoured ambulance and troop carrier, based on the chassis of NIMRÓD at the training camp at Esztergom-tábor, summer 1943. The original Swedish L-62's chassis was used for tests. The complete superstructure and the turret was removed, the front armour was increased with welded plate, the headlight and the fan were also removed and their holes were covered with armour plates. Even the driver's cupola was missing while the test vehicle made its driving tests on the training ground at Esztergom-tábor. There is a frame for a tarpaulin on the superstructure. The students of the Ludovika Military Academy's tank company examine the new fighting vehicle.

Attila Bonhardt

The final version of the LEHEL's prototype in the yard of the Institute of Military Technology. The turret was replaced by an open-topped (tarpaulin covered), lengthened superstructure in which stretchers could be placed. The driver's cupola was also partly integrated into the superstructure. The left visor slit of the driver was cut onto the superstructure's sidewall. Here we can see the superstructure uncovered, the tarpaulin is hanging on its frame in the middle. Note the holders of the tarpaulin and the 'L'-shaped straps on the side of the vehicle.

Front view of the LEHEL. The armour plates above the openings of the headlight and the fan are clearly seen on the increased front plate. The two small position lights were replaced by two bigger headlights without any protection, which were fixed to both sides of the driving compartment instead of the mudguards. Note the electric horn on the right front plate of the superstructure (same as on the ZRÍNYI assault howitzer). Significant changes were made to the driver's compartment. Although the cupola was still openable to the right side for better visibility, the driver couldn't use it as a hatch as the superstructure was lengthened. The driver could get in or out of the vehicle through the fighting compartment.

Attila Bonhardt

Rear view of the LEHEL's ambulance version. There were places for two stretchers above each other inside for four patients. The middle section of the rear plate was foldable, and two rails helped the handling of the stretchers. We can see the speedometer between the two stretchers. The cover fan of the ventilator moved inside because of the lengthened superstructure. Note the small details of the rear wall and the engine deck, and the large national insignia.